The Odd Squad GUIDE TO POO

Why you should never ask
the barber for a number two.

by Becky & Allan Plenderleith

ЯR
RAVETTE PUBLISHING

For Daniel & Stuart

The Odd Squad and all related characters © 2009
Created by Allan Plenderleith
www.allanplenderleith.com

Visit The Odd Squad's Shoppy Shop at
www.zazzle.co.uk/oddsquad

Previously entitled The Odd Squad's Big Poo Handbook

First published in 2009
Reprinted 2012, 2013, 2014

This edition first published in 2017 by Ravette Publishing Limited
PO Box 876, Horsham, West Sussex RH12 9GH
info@ravettepub.co.uk

ISBN: 978-1-84161-400-7

May the farts be with you ... always.

Printed and bound in India by Replika Press Pvt. Ltd.

A BRIEF HISTORY OF POO!

orget school/university/grandparent versions of history. hokum pokum. Lies, damned lies. They don't want you to know The Truth. But we don't give a stuff. here's what <u>really</u> happened in the anals of history...

THE BIG BANG

Chemicals swirling around in one explosive cocktail? Pah! One day God was on the crapper after a night out on the clouds and, woosh, got the trots. Nine poops later and the solar system was formed, the sun being God's red-sore sphincter!

god's anus

uranus

The DINOSAUR AGE

Finally the truth about the extinction of dinosaurs! As they became bigger and bigger, so did their poos. Soon they were up to their necks in their own bum sludge. In the baking heat it soon hardened around them, trapping them there until they died. Stupid lizards.

The DAWN OF MAN

Millions of years later, when monkeys were throwing their own banana-scented faeces at themselves, one particular ape refused to touch his own poo, preferring to wipe his bum with a palm leaf and spray the air with magnolia pollen — and mankind was born!

The EGYPTIANS

Civilised society the Egyptians – they had a penchant for Toblerone. However, this resulted in triangular poos (no wonder they walked funny). Lacking a decent sewage system, the Egyptian wideboy Tootandcomin (so called because he would always fart before he asked people to 'come in') ordered his people to stack their poos somewhere in the desert. The resulting poop pile became the wonderful pyramids!

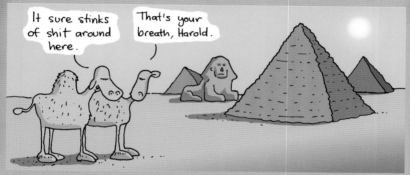

The VIKINGS

Often falsely accused of being 'hairy horny marauders' the Vikings were actually soft pansies with a fondness for synchronised rowing with a poor sense of direction getting lost often (blondes you see). They were too girly to 'log overboard' so they had to wait until they reached land then run screaming with bulging pants to the nearest settlement, scaring the crap out of the locals.

1066 The Battle of Poostings

Two silly armies of men were fighting about who took the last sheet of loo roll when King Harold got struck in the eye by a U.F.O. (Unusual Faecal Obelisk) and after a rather nasty eye infection, died of embarrassment.

The Brownish-Black Plague

The story goes that Marco Polo, from his travels in the Far East, brought back the world's first Chinese takeaway. By the time it reached our shores, however, the sweet and sour "chicken" with fried rice was heaving with disease, but divvy Marco foolishly warmed it up in the oven and ate it anyway. Soon Marco ran into the street screaming with Brownish Black diarrhoea spraying out of his behind. The deadly disease spread across Europe like a DJ Otzi record. Many died.

1666 The Great Poo of London

It started in Smeggy Lane, at a Baker's when the Youth Training
Scheme lad forgot to wash his hands after squeezing his zits.
Then he made a batch of YumYums which sold like hot doughnuts,
triggering a snowball effect of upset tummies. People were
pooping directly onto the pavements and into each others' pockets.
But then, Mrs Cawley lit a match to deal with all that gas and
toxic fumes. Boom! (NB: London still smells of poo to this day!)

1920's POOhIBITION

In America during the trotting twenties, people were pooing far
too much, so the president of the time, Jimmy Carter, decided
to ban pooping. But this merely encouraged mafia-like poop-legging
where people would pay to go on illicit buckets under the moonshine.

1969 First Poo on the Moon

Neil Arsestrong was the first man to lay a cable on another planet. Apparently Neil's poos looked remarkably similar to golden eagles, hence the phrase: 'The Eagle has landed.' As Neil stepped onto the planet for the first time, he released an enormous poop, uttering the immortal line: 'One small step for man, one giant poop for mankind.'

1980's Poo Mountains

As a consequence of famine in third world countries, there was a shortage of poo in these undeveloped zones. Thankfully, the well-fed developed world stepped in, shipping huge mountains of western excrement to supplement their poop drought. Aren't we kind!

THE TEN POO COMMANDMENTS

1. Thou shalt not kill off a turd mid-delivery!

2. Thou shalt not steal the last sheet of toilet roll without replacing it – unless, of course, you are in a friend's house!

3. Thou shalt not covet another man's turds!

4. Thou shalt not commit adultery with another man's toilet!

5. Thou shalt not take the Turd's name in vain!

6. Thou shalt not poo on a Sunday!

7. Thou shalt not disrespect thy mother and father's incontinence!

8. Thou shalt not give false evidence to thy neighbour!

9. Thou shalt not have any other turds than me!

10. Thou shalt not construct effigies in my image!

Poo in the Arts

Poo has been an inspiration to artists for centuries: from the early drawings of cavemen having a dump (hmm, wonder what they used for paint?) to every entry in the Turner Prize. So let's take a stroll through the anals of art history.

The Moaning Lisa

Many have pondered upon the reason behind 'The Moaning Lisa's' strange expression. Has she managed to lay a 3 foot cable without it breaking off? Has the splash from a malteser poo just gone up her bum? Or has she got piles? We will never know. Displayed in the Loo Gallery in Paris.

Moaning Lisa

Poos in Clouds

An early work by Money, a part-time toilet attendant. He found there wasn't a big demand for paintings of the filthy poo-ridden rivers of France, so went on to paint pretty pictures of lily-pads instead.

(though if the paint is stripped off you will find poops sneakily painted underneath)

Poo in Formaldehyde

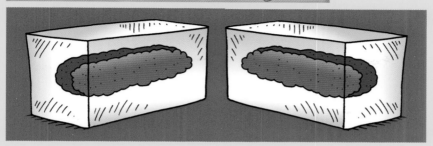

Millionaire artist Damien 'Omen' Hearse created huge controversy (and piles of cash) with this piece. Some say it's about 'society's duality when confronted with the truth of existence'. Others think it's just crap.

Andy Sorehole's Poo Copies

Wacky white-haired Sorehole thought that photocopying pictures of poo and colouring them in with crayon was really clever, suggesting that although we all think we are unique individuals, our poos are all identical and therefore we are all part of a greater 'oneness'. But that's rubbish! We all know every poo is completely different like those sweetcorn ones, or the ones with jaggy bits or the ones that you need to wipe forever...

Poo in Unmade Bed

Vodka-breath 'artist' Tracey Eminem came up with this effort after a big night on the Liefraumilch. She awoke to find the heap still steaming on the sheets but claims it wasn't hers (yeah, right). Some fool bought it for a million which she spent immediately on a Smirnoff factory.

Poocasso's Log

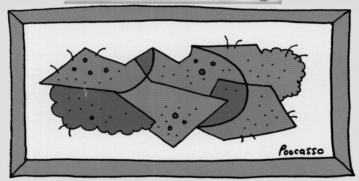

Sitting on the loo wondering what he could cut off to make himself famous in the art world, Poocasso dropped this baby down the pan. Once he (and his sphincter) had recovered from the shock, the poo's bizarre shape inspired him to create a new art form - cubism! All that from simply eating too many crisps!

Dali's Melted Poos

Salivate Dali, the Spanish painter, was extremely fond of garlic. The problem was his breath was absolutely rank (even curling his moustache) and consequently everything he tried to paint actually melted, hence the famous 'melted poos'. His career ended when one day he accidentally ate a tic tac.

Henry Poore

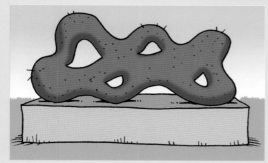

Henry Poore, the English sculptor, was addicted to curly wurlies. So much so that his poos began to resemble the twisted chocolate treat. He produced large sculptures of these master poos. Academics thought they looked like women and stuff, and bingo - he made the big time!

Jackson Bollock

The world's worst artist, Jackson Bollock, was so bad at art he actually pooed on his own artwork in frustration. Unfortunately, one poncey art critic saw the result, hailed it a masterpiece by a troubled mind (troubled sphincter more like!), and subsequently Jackson was deemed a genius. He wasn't. He was just an ordinary guy with a sore arse.

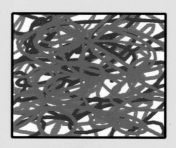

JACKSON BOLLOCK

HMM, I SEE EIGHT PINTS OF LAGER, CHEAP ALCOPOPS AND A DODGY KEBAB.

The Inspooration BEHIND
the Inventions!

For centuries, mankind has attributed the world's greatest inventions to the selfless desire by the brilliant few to improve the quality of life for the masses. Pff! It's all about crapping...

FIRE (21 July something BC)

Caveman Uga Booga invented fire as he idly rubbed two twigs together waiting for a bout of constipation to pass (all those herbivorian banquets) and realised it was also an hilarious way to maximise fart entertainment!

THE TELEPHONE (1876)

Sir Alexander Graham Bell invented the telephone so that we can ring our friends and brag about the size of our poops. Nowadays we use the phone to call our friends when we know that they'll be mid-strain on the loo, eg: 8am and 2.47pm. Ha!

The LIGHTBULB (1879)

Thomas Edison invented the lightbulb to encourage people not to poop in the wrong place in the dark of the night. Killjoy.

The AIRPLANE (1903)

Orville (yes, the duck - he's always been interested in flying, right up to the sky) and Wilbur Wright invented the first passenger aircraft to enable them to fly over conurbations and drop poo bombs on unsuspecting passers-by. And you thought that was bird crap on your car.

The TELEVISION (1926)

Saint John Logie Baird invented the television to help us pass the time between craps. Join the crusade to have him canonized now.

The LAVATORY (1876)

Thomas Crapper invented the toilet as a private health spa for poos with plunge pool, pine aromatherapy treatments and Jacuzzi.

THE 7 DEADLY POO SINS

1.
NEVER CROSS A PARK IN HIGH HEELS!

2.
NEVER ROLL DOWN A HILL WITH CAREFREE ABANDON!

3.
NEVER BEND BACK TOO FAR TO SMELL YOUR OWN FARTS!

4.
BEFORE BLOWING OFF IN SHORTS, ALWAYS MAKE SURE IT'S NOT A WET ONE!

5.
NEVER HOLD YOUR POOS IN FOR TOO LONG!

6.
NEVER FOLLOW THROUGH IN THE SWIMMING BATHS!

7.
NEVER BLOW OFF WHILST IN THE DOGGY POSITION

The Odd Squad's Guide to POO

'THE FIREBALL'

HOT AND PAINFUL.
MAY SINGE
BOTTOM HAIRS.

'THE CHOP OFF'

POO IS STOPPED
HALF-WAY DUE TO
PHONE RINGING ETC.

'THE SWEETCORN'

MOST COLOURFUL
AND ATTRACTIVE.

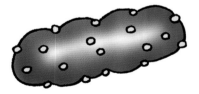

'THE JAGGY'

CAUSED BY EATING
TOO MANY CRISPS.
MAY RESULT IN
SURGERY.

'THE STICKY'
STICKS TO HAIRS. REQUIRES HOURS OF WIPING.

'THE VEGGIE'
LOOKS AND SMELLS EXACTLY LIKE A VEGGIE BURGER.

'THE FIREHOSE'
MAINLY WATER-BASED. CREATES HUGE MESS.

'THE CROQUETTES'
CRISPY ON THE OUTSIDE WITH A LIGHT, PUFFY CENTRE.

'THE NEVERENDING STORY'
AN AMAZING ACHIEVEMENT. MAY NEED TO STAND TO ACCOMPLISH FULL LENGTH.

'THE BLIP'
SMALL BUT CAUSES BIG SPLASH.

'THE SLIPPY'

SLIPS OUT IN ONE, SWIFT
MOVEMENT. REQUIRES
NO WIPING.

"THE STINKER'

REEKS SO BAD YOU
DON'T EVEN RECOGNISE
THE SMELL.

'THE POPPETS'

COME OUT LIKE MACHINE
GUN BULLETS.

'THE STEAMY HEAPY'

WILL NEVER FLUSH.

THE KLINGON!

BECOMES TRAPPED
IN BOTTOM HAIRS.
MUST BE REMOVED
WITH FINGERS.
NICE!

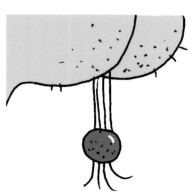

THE GREAT TAKEAWAY FOOD POO TEST!

THE CHINESE MEAL POO

NICE AT THE TIME BUT ULTIMATELY UNSATISFYING. YOU'LL FEEL LIKE ANOTHER ONE IN HALF AN HOUR.

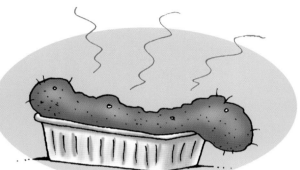

THE MCBURGER POO

DRY, OVERCOOKED, AND EACH POO IS IDENTICAL. WARNING: MAY CONTAIN TEENAGE STAFF'S BOGIES!

THE FISH & CHIPS POO

A SUCCULENT POO WITH A CRISPY OUTER COATING. FOLLOWED BY A SIDE PORTION OF MUSHY PEA POO!

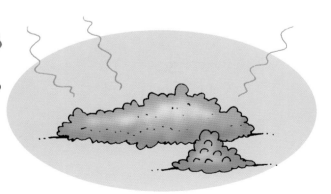

THE INDIAN MEAL POO

A REAL ARSE BURNER.
SITTING DOWN WILL
BE IMPOSSIBLE
FOR WEEKS. KEEP
FIRE EXTINGUISHER
HANDY.

THE DODGY BURGER VAN POO

THE FASTEST
POO IN THE WEST.
FOOD GOES FROM
MOUTH TO BUM IN
3.5 MINUTES DUE TO
99% GERM CONTENT.
SMELLS OF
WET ONIONS.

THPPPPPPPPTT!!!!!

THE KEBAB POO

FOUL-SMELLING,
SLIMY, GROTESQUE
APPEARANCE.
JUST LIKE A
KEBAB, REALLY!

HOW YOUR POOS CHANGE AS YOU GET OLDER!

BABY POO

LIKE NUCLEAR CABBAGE ONLY MORE DEADLY. DO NOT LET IT COME IN CONTACT WITH SKIN.

TEENAGE POO

JUST A BIG BALL OF LARD. MADE FROM A DIET OF BURGERS, PIZZAS AND CHOCOLATE. HIGHLY INFECTIOUS.

TWENTY SOMETHING POO

POO IS GREEN DUE TO SUDDEN HEALTH KICK. BUT MORE VEG IN DIET MEANS SMELLIER POOS.

THIRTYSOMETHING POO

AN INCREASE IN DINNER PARTIES MEANS POOS BECOME DARKER AND RICHER IN QUALITY. THE BOUQUET IS ALMOST PLEASANT.

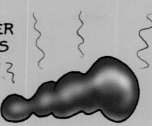

FORTYSOMETHING POO

MIDDLE AGE SPREAD SETS IN. POOS BECOME HUGE, SWOLLEN MONSTROSITIES. JUST LIKE THEIR BIG ARSES.

O.A.P. (Old Aged Poo)

POOS ARE GREY, WRINKLY, DRIED UP, AND SMELL LIKE ROTTING FLESH. JUST LIKE AN OLD PERSON REALLY!

The Odd Squad's
Greatest Shits

JUDGING BY ALL THE
CHOCOLATE KISSES ON THE FLOOR,
THE DOG'S BUM WAS
IN NEED OF A WASH AGAIN.

UNFORTUNATELY, DUG
HAD EATEN ONE TOO MANY
CURLY WURLIES

ONCE AGAIN,
BILLY'S GOLDFISH HAD
DIARRHOEA

BILLY COMES FIRST IN THE
SWIMMING CONTEST THANKS
TO LILY'S VINDALOO

APPARENTLY, THE DOG
HAD SWALLOWED AN
ICING BAG NOZZLE

JEFF ENTERS ANOTHER
'WIPE IT OR LEAVE IT'
DILEMMA

MAUDE DISCOVERS
SHE HAS V.P.L. (VISIBLE
POO LINE)

BILLY'S PET WORM, CYRIL,
WAS CONSTIPATED AGAIN

Poo Myths

if you don't wash your hands after you've been to the toilet you will get stomach ache.

FACT

incorrect. you <u>will</u> get a fashionable brown shade of nail varnish!

if you watch your partner going for a dump, they will lose their romantic allure.

FACT

chances are, they've already lost it (especially if you've been together for more than 2 weeks)

 **Myth:** if you have diarrhoea you must replace lost fluids with plenty of water.

 **FACT**

Nah. don't bother. It's the only time you'll experience that mr. universe muscle definition!

If he doesn't drink soon he'll die.

Yeah, but look at those abs!

 **Myth:** if you try to look between your legs to watch yourself dumping and the wind changes, you'll stay that way.

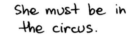 **FACT**

It's true actually! try it!

She must be in the circus.

 **Myth:** if you strain too hard, you will get piles.

FACT

False. but your innards may be forced out.

Phone the doctor.

R.C. TRAVEL GUIDE TO UK PUBLIC CONVENIENCES

Coloombus, Ridley Scott of the Antarsetic, Sore Walter Raleigh...travellers and explorers who braved uncharted lands in search of clean places to poop. They've all gone. So here's a dodgy guide to local WCs to do the dirty (few backhanders were accepted in the making of this guide).

McBURGER CHAINS

FACILITIES

The bare minimum. Several cubicles featuring single WC suites - though a number will be either blocked, impressively filthy, or the door engagingly broken or occupied by old ladies who can't lock the door. En suite basins will feature scalding water and sticky soap that never washes off. Hand dryers, if electric, feature a micro laboratory of deadly germ warfare; or the towel roll will already be strangely soaking; or individual paper towel dispenser will tantalisingly feature a small triangle of paper that you just can't pull. Single sex rooms only and women's options will feature sanitary bins that are overflowing. Men's option will be flooded... but not with water.

LOCATION

...its only plus. These bog standard facilities are everywhere - with the added bonus that you can eat whilst you defecate.

Turd rating:

PUBLIC TOILETS

FACILITIES

Usually Victorian in design, prehistoric in sanitation, "Gentlemen's" urinals will feature the discolouration of an alcoholic, toffee-eating smoker and curious holes drilled in the side panels of cubicles. Whilst the "Ladies" will feature scary, elevated cubicle side doors from where ghostly hands appear begging for paper (that's if you've made it through the pain barrier of old granny piss stench). ★

LOCATION

The usual hunting ground for the above - car parks and lonely scenic spots in local parks. Only recommended for use if you are an adrenalin junkie.

*Public Conveniences are very popular choices with gay men and murderers. Special offers may be available.

Turd rating: MINUS

SHOPPING CENTRE

FACILITIES

The usual... broken cubicles, splashed toilet seats, mis-spelt graffiti but with the additional service of piped music to cover the splattering sound effects of fellow customers. You may also enjoy the added excitement of thick people trying to open your door despite the lock clearly displaying an "Engaged" notice. Also features an idle attendant who appears to be physically unable to flush offending floaters ('offending' only because they're not your own). Revel in the huge smudge-ridden mirrors featuring teenage girls daubing their eyes in kohl, and teenage boys squeezing their zits.

LOCATION

Always the furthest possible distance when you realise you're wetting yourself, regardless of where you are. Turd rating:

PUBLIC HOUSES

FACILITIES

Like home from home - very comfy surrounds with carpet, curtains and the over-use of air fresheners to mask the permanent aroma of beer, puke and fags. Customers may also enjoy the added luxury of a condom machine (though you will have to provide your own partner). Or an American-tan tight machine (though you may not have the old lady legs to properly display them).

LOCATION

In towns and cities, approx every 30 drunken stumbles, but you may feel the need to purchase an alcoholic beverage (or ten) to alleviate your guilt over abusing their facilities for "patrons only" (oh well). Alternatively, run like the wind past landlord. In villages and hamlets, you may experience "the locals" syndrome. Nettle-ridden roadside verges suddenly seem a welcoming option.

Turd rating:

HARRUDS

FACILITIES

Yeah, yeah, very nice gold plating
but is any poop worth £1 a shot??!!
Erm, well yes! Poops deserve the best!

LOCATION

No idea. Ask a tourist.

Turd rating:

DISABLED TOILETS

FACILITIES

Ahhhh, the crème de la crème of crappers.
Spacious, clean facilities that have only
ever been used 3 times before. Low level
hand bars are excellent for gripping on to
during constipation. And an emergency
button should you require room service.

LOCATION

Surprisingly available all over the place.

Turd rating:

TOILETS AT OUTDOOR MUSIC FESTIVALS

FACILITIES

Everything the professional crapper needs:
day-long queues to help build-up
pleasure for eventual ejection; opportunity
to spot/admire rival turtleheads; develop
resourcefulness when it comes to wiping
derrière with... apparently, nothing; the
sheer thrill of not being able to 'go' when
it's finally your turn; hand washer in the
form of a pikey's dog... The list is endless -
just like the endless diarrhoea you get
free from the dodgy hippie burger stall.

LOCATION

Just follow the holy pilgrimage of sewage.

Turd rating:

POO SUPERSTITIONS

Humans are a supoostitous bunch, always looking for 'signs'. But these are indeed based on scientific fact and not female PMT witchery...

WALKING UNDER A LADDER

It IS bad luck, the workman atop the ladder is actually quite likely to poo whilst he's up there, as the poo slips so easily out of his visible builder's cleavage.

'STEP ON A CRACK BREAK YOUR MOTHER'S BACK'

This is true. As you trip over the crack and fall you'll grab your ageing mother and she'll go flying.

AAEEE

LUCKY HORSEPOOS

Hang a horsepoo over your doorway and ye shall have good luck - salesmen and tory candidates won't come anywhere near your house!

WELCOME

UMBRELLAS INDOORS

Opening an umbrella indoors is actually lucky because fart gas will be trapped in the umbrella, letting you savour your guff for longer!

mmmm!

'BREAK A TURD AND IT'S 7 YEARS BAD LUCK'

We need to raise the ceiling in here!

Absolutely true. It's a henous crime to break off long intestinal turds in mid-flow as they only materialise once every seven years.

Poo Hair Dos

Poo has a far-retching influence in all aspects of everyday life. Even hair fashions - as seen recently on the catwalks of Pooris, Poo York and Poolan... It won't be long before everyone's asking for Jennifer Aniston's Rectal!

The Rectal

Long, flat, super-glossy turds that have been tamed with straightening irons and enhanced by a carb-free diet. Basically, the runs.

The Pellet

As modelled by celebrities such as Craig David and, er, Hamble.

The Princess Lay-a-Poo

Feel the force as you squeeze out these two perfect Cumberlands, attach to head with strawberry jam.

The Gareth Gates

Follow the 2-1-2 formation, cement with something wet and shiny, and the screaming will soon follow.

The Rapunzel

A look mostly worn by old ladies who are unaware that they're going to the poo, and also, too infirm to break off and wipe the detritus.

The Mohican Skid

A touching look worn by guys who lift their girlfriends on to their shoulders at music concerts.

The Beckham

Long or short, it doesn't matter, so long as your mousy barnet is crowned with yellow streaks (just eat plenty of custard).

The Constipator

When everything's backed up down there, go sans hair for that Eastend hardnut/Gayboy look!

Poo Tips
for the busy housewife!

PROBLEM:
Plagued by the vanishing turd? Feel cheated by its callous disappearing act?

SOLUTION:
Pad the plunge pool with ecologically-unfriendly amounts of loo roll to cushion its fall and present itself to you like a play-bunny on silken sheets.

PROBLEM:
Is your husband constantly leaving the lavatory seat up, causing you untold emotional distress as your derrière meets cold wet ceramic?

SOLUTION:
Divorce.

PROBLEM:
Is your wife constantly leaving the lavatory seat up, causing you serious back strain with the constant lifting of disturbingly clean seats?

SOLUTION:
Cheat on her with a blonde bimbo.

PROBLEM:
Do you experience an irrational desire to use public conveniences whenever you see one, despite hating them?

SOLUTION:
Pants can withstand a moist turtlehead longer than you may imagine. Instead, visit an expensive restaurant for a superfluous meal and use their more uplifting facilities.

PROBLEM:
Does someone keep leaving pubes on the toilet seat?

SOLUTION:
Lucky you. Fashion the hairs into a mirkin and sell on the black market!

DOCTOR DI O'RHEA
for all your toilet troubles!

PATIENT: I can't stop imagining the Queen on the toilet. What's wrong with me?

Dr. O'Rhea: Nothing. Me too.

PATIENT: My wife says it's worth the extra 30p for premium toilet roll, is she right? Wouldn't cheaper, recycled paper be better for the planet?

Get a grip. Over the course of your lifetime, you're wasting £3984 on posh paper — that's the same as a 40inch plasma telly!

Every time I go for a whoopsie all I produce are perfectly formed rabbit droppings. It's so boring! What's up Doc?

Dr. O'Rhea: Hoppit!

PATIENT: You're my last resort. My boyfriend's driving me nuts with his inability to leave the toilet seat UP. What's wrong with him?

Dr. O'Rhea: Durr, he's gay.

Patient: I have a phobia about dropping my load in my friend's house in case I leave a smear. Any suggestions?

Dr. O'Rhea: Why not start a profitable business as a pebble dash exterior specialist.

Patient: Please help me. What can I do about my two-foot turds that just won't flush away?

Dr. O'Rhea: Lucky git. Peddle your talents as a mini tourist attraction- advertise that the Loch Ness Monster has had babies!

Patient: My wife is obsessed with the bidet - she spends hours cleaning herself 'down there'. Is she a cleaning compulsive?

Dr. O'Rhea: No. Just sexually satisfied.

Patient: I'm secretly disgusted by my girlfriend - every time I get jiggy with her I can't help but notice the skids in her G-string. Should I 'dump' her?!

Dr. O'Rhea: Not necessarily. This information makes excellent blackmail material – steal a pair for future 'negotiations'!

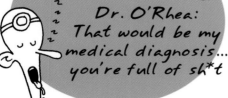

Patient: I've heard the colon can store pounds of poo – is that why I'm overweight?

Dr. O'Rhea: That would be my medical diagnosis... you're full of sh*t

Patient: Is anal sex a bit like having a great dump?

Dr. O'Rhea: I plead the 5th amendment!

A day in the life of a POO

by Alfred J. Poo
the turd x

My day begins around 8am when I begin wriggling in the intestinal tract of my human host (or 'parasite' as I like to call them). I find wriggling an effective way of generating gurgling, thus tricking my host into thinking they're starving and need breakfast. You see, I like a big fry up – all that grease oils the tubes for my 'parcel-force delivery.' And all that nosh weighs heavy on their bowel. So hoorah, there's nowhere for me to go but to my private swimming pool. After bidding "adieu" to my neighbours, L.Casei Immunitas (my, they're a friendly bunch), I put on my very fashionable sweetcorn swimsuit and do a 'bomber' off the diving board ... I think you humans call it an anus!

WEEEEEEE!

I love the adrenalin rush of the freefall – I just pray my pool isn't too clean. There's nothing worse to a poop than a pool full of bleach and lemon-scented Toilet Muck™. Ugh. If I'm feeling mischievous, I'll dive straight into the U-bend, thereby depriving my host the privilege of admiring their deposit. Tee hee! But more often than not, I'll practise my "Dead Goldfish" synchronised swimming movement. Also, call me kinky but I'm quite keen on receiving the golden shower that usually accompanies splashdown. Being dirty's in my genes I guess! But ironically, the whole experience can be just like a spa treatment – being hosed down by a urinary jet, then covered in warm, muddy blankets of loo roll. I prefer recycled because then I can fantasise about where it's been!!

Then, the 'Jacuzzi' gets turned on as my proud host reluctantly pulls the flusher. Weeheeeee! Round and round I spin in an eddy of peey bubbles. If I've been good (over-indulged and put on weight), I won't disappear the first time, which means I can indulge in a spot of S&M. Ooh-er missus! I love being beaten with the bog brush. All those bristles. Ouch. Ooh. The climax for me is to be spanked so hard, I break in two - then I'll have a companion for the day, my genetic clone!

Next, it's time for the water park - those sewer chutes are wicked. Twisting and turning, what a high. And the smell? Heaven! I may meet a few old friends along the way... Grandpa Constipation Nugget clinging for dear fossilised life on the brickwork... Or that slapper, Aunty Diarrhoea spreading herself about a bit (nothing changes!).

Sometimes I'll make new pals, I still keep in touch with Nathan the Alligator who was flushed when he got too big. Nice dude. A bit needy. I'll float on my back for a while, practise my "Jaws" impersonation. I'd love to appear on "Stars in their Arse". Well, a turd can dream. But I'll come crashing back to earth when I arrive at my destination. It's paradise to me, though – the coast off Seaton Carew. Bliss. The water's beautiful... icy cold (brings a youthful flushed tone to my skin), salty (excellent for skin complaints like turd fissures) and, most importantly of all, full of pollution. What more could a jobby ask for?

The End!

NEXT WEEK:
A day in the life
of a Colostomy Bag!

The A to Z of Poo!

A is for arse

REGULAR   J-LO

B is for **bottyburps**

UUURP!!

Excuse me.

C is for **constipation**

D is for **diarrhoea**

E is for **eye-watering**

NNN GGG!

F is for floater

G is for groan

H is for hairy

I is for iceberg

J is for jaw-dropper

K is for Krakatoa

L is for log

M is for moist wipe

N is for no-show

O is for OUCH!

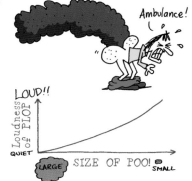

P is for plop!

Q is for quake

R is for rabbit droppings

S is for splashback

T is for talented

U is for unexpected

V is for vanishing poo

W is for wipe, wipe, wipe, wipe...

X is for xmas poo

Y is for yo-yo

Z is for zombie poo (done by old ladies)

Cinderella

nce upon a grime-covered toilet, Cinders (so-called because she once over-enthusiastically lit her own fart) was scrubbing away, dreaming of going to the ball. But there was fat chance of that as her bulimic step-sisters had made a right mess of the loo and it was taking forever to clean. Yet, loo and behold, the Fairly Bogmother appeared in a spray of air freshener and told Cinders she was going to the ball! Waving her magic bog brush, she transformed Cinders' rags into a Versarses number and turned the loo roll into a Lootus.

However, at the ball Cinders was so excited to be asked to dance by the inbred Prince that she pooped herself and ran off. The impressed Prince picked up the poop and scoured the land in search of its owner. Eventually he found Maude and, lo, the poo fit her bum hole perfectly! But the marriage only lasted 3 months as it turned out the prince was actually a raving woofter.

THE END!

Little Red Riding Hood

One fine day Little Red Riding Hood was walking through the woods to visit her boring grandmother when she skidded in a turd left by an inconsiderate wolf, breaking her neck. Serves her right - hoods are soooo last spring!

THE END!

The Princess and the Poo

No wonder I couldn't sleep! Although my back feels better.

A month ago, a Princess was staying in a dodgy B&B and couldn't get to sleep - what with the smell of old smoke and sex, the polyester stained top blanket and the fear of the morning cuppa from the hospitality tray made with mini cartons of foul milk - oh, and best not forget to mention the lumpy mattress, the reason for the whole story!

So the Princess pulled back the mattress to discover a poop left by the previous occupant. Charming. In the morning, when the maids were spraying the sheets with freshener, they discovered their favourite mattress poop had been stolen. But all the mini toiletries that reeked of pine disinfectant were still there!

THE END!

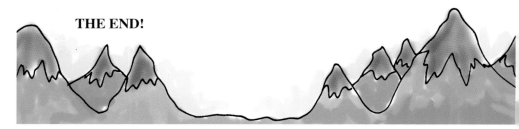

Goldilocks and the 3 Bears

n a land, fart fart away, Goldilocks was in the forest looking for truffles to flog to poncey restaurants when the urge to dump over-whelmed her... Fortunately, there was a house nearby she could break into, so Goldilocks shimmied up the drainpipe and climbed in through an open window.

The first toilet she came to was a potty, so she whisked her knicks off and shouted "Timber", but the potty was way too small for her big ass so she had to waddle to the next room, where she found a urinal.   But it wasn't in the right position and Goldilocks ended up making a mess. So she waddled to the next room, where she found the perfect toilet... three empty porridge bowls!

THE END (of the bears!)

POO IN THE MOVIES

BEHIND EVERY GREAT FILM IS AN EVEN GREATER STORY ABOUT POO THAT THE STUDIOS THOUGHT WAS JUST TOO POWERFUL/RADICAL/TOUCHING/SEXY TO MAKE. JUST WHERE DID YOU THINK THE INSPIRATION FOR THE DESIGN OF POPCORN CAME FROM!?...

THE DAMBUSTERS

1945. A BUNCH OF ENGLISHMEN WERE IN GERMANY FOR A BEER FESTIVAL AND DECIDED TO BROWN-BOMB THE TOILETS. THE LAGER-FUELLED CANNON BALLS WERE TOO STRONG FOR THE LOCAL LOOS AND BOUNCED THEIR WAY TO THE RESERVOIR WHERE THEY SMASHED THE DAM, CAUSING A HUGE FLOOD.
SO THANKS TO POO WE WON THE WAR!

GONE WITH THE WIND

A FRIGID GIRL WOULDN'T BE WITH THE MAN OF HER DREAMS JUST BECAUSE HE HAD CHRONIC FLATULENCE. BUT HE DIDN'T WANT TO BE WITH HER EITHER BECAUSE HER CRINOLINE WAS ALWAYS GETTING CAUGHT IN HER SUSPICIOUSLY LESS-THAN-WHITE PANTALOONS.

(HISTORY LESSON: CRINOLINES MADE IT IMPOSSIBLE TO POO QUICKLY, THEREFORE PANTALOONS WERE INVENTED TO STORE WEEKS' WORTH OF POO)

JAWS

A MIDDLE-AGED POLICEMAN CAN'T BE BOTHERED TO GO BACK TO SHORE TO RELIEVE HIMSELF SO HE DROPS HIS LOAD IN THE SEA. HOWEVER, IT TERRORISES THE SPINELESS LOCALS AS IT BOBS MERRILY ALONG, UNINTENTIONALLY KILLING OFF SEVERAL BATHERS WITH STOMACH INFECTIONS.

CITIZEN KANE

MAN BUYS NEWSPAPER THAT HE CALLS "THE BUM" SO HE CAN PRINT PAGE AFTER PAGE OF GRATUITOUS NAKED CRAP. IT'S BRILLIANT.

THE WIZARD OF OZ

"HEALTHY EATER" (IE. SHE HAD AN EATING DISORDER) DOROTHY PASSES OUT WHILST STRAINING IN CONSTIPATED AGONY. UNCONSCIOUS, SHE DREAMS OF VISITING A WIZARD WHO CAN GIVE HER A TURD. ON THE WAY SHE MEETS A LION WITHOUT A SPHINCTER AND A TIN MAN WITHOUT A FART (THE SCARECROW DIED IN A FREAK FART-LIGHTING ACCIDENT). WHEN SHE WAKES UP DOROTHY DISCOVERS SHE'S POOPED THE BED.

THE TEXAS CHAINSAW MASSACRE

A GANG OF FREE-LOADING STUDENTS
ON A LONG JOURNEY ALL NEED A
POO AFTER A NIGHT ON THE CIDER,
SO THEY BREAK INTO A HOUSE TO
USE THE TOILET WITHOUT PERMISSION...
LITTLE DO THEY KNOW IT BELONGS TO
AN AGORAPHOBIC AND IT'S HER
TIME OF THE MONTH! IT'S A
BLOODBATH!

LORD OF THE RINGS

A DOCUMENTARY ABOUT A HAIRY
SHORT-ARSE WHO MUST PROTECT
HIS SPECIAL RING BEFORE TWO
PERVY OLD SORCERORS
GET THEIR FILTHY HANDS ON IT.

THE GODFATHER

COMEDY ABOUT THE TURTLE-HEAD
OF THE ITALIAN 'CORLEONE' FAMILY
WHO RUN A LAUNDERING RACKET.
NOT MONEY LAUNDERING,
BUT ACTUAL LAUNDERING
OF BED SHEETS, SOILED
BY PEOPLE FORCED TO EAT
CORLEONE'S DODGY LASAGNES.

CHITTY CHITTY BANG BANG

THE CHARMING STORY OF A FAMILY OFF TO THE ZOO IN THE CAR WHEN GRANNY NEEDS HER YEARLY DUMP. THEY SPEND THE DAY LOOKING FOR A VERGE BUT EVENTUALLY SHE RESORTS TO POOPING IN THE FUEL TANK - THE FUMES ARE SO GASEOUS THE CAR EXPLODES, FLYING THROUGH THE AIR. ORIGINALLY CALLED "SHITTY SHITTY BANG BANG."

THE TERMINATOR

AN OLD BIDDY WHO DOESN'T KNOW HOW TO USE THE NO-TOUCH ELECTRONIC FLUSH MECHANISM ON A HIGH-TECH TOILET AND LEAVES A FLOATER, RESULTING IN THE PEEVED-OFF LOO ATTENDANT CHASING HER.

THE SIXTH SENSE

SPOOKY TOSH ABOUT A YOUNG BOY WHO CLAIMS "I CAN SEE POO PEOPLE". APPARENTLY WHEN OUR POOS ARE FLUSHED THEY DON'T DIE, THEY HANG AROUND IN SPIRIT FORM, HAUNTING US. SO THAT'S WHAT THAT FUNNY SMELL IS.

A TOUCHING GUIDE FOR
New Poorents

Everything You Always Wanted To Know About
Human Repooduction But Were Too Ladyboy To Ask

How are poobies made? Tee hee!
Does it hurt the first time? (If you're lucky it should hurt every time)
Will there be blood? (Yes, if you try hard enough)
Should you always use protection... against splashback? (Men prefer not to)
What makes sextuplets? (Who cares - you can sell your story to a tabloid,
or give them up for adoption)

Haven't the foggiest. But we do know what happens after a prune and
a cabbage see each other across a crowded stomach and sneak off to get
jiggy in the alimentary canal...

What To Expect in Delivery

If you've been good you'll experience hours of sublime pain, followed by a
few seconds of slippery relief as you jettison your special little guy in to
your partner's arms. But middle-class hygiene-fixated trendies prefer
old-fashioned water births (down the pan). There may or may not be a
mucous cord attached to your new offspring which can be severed with
scissors or your fingers. Many couples like to make a home movie of this
wonderful event - you can make a lotta money on the internet.

Oh God, it's ugly!
Suck it back in!

AAEEEEE!!

Immediately After Delivery

Swaddle your new-born in
luxurious loo paper, though
if it is less attractive than
you were hoping for, cheap
stuff will serve it right.

She's got your eyes.

Sharing Your Delight With Family
And Friends And Passers-by
(Or How To Turn Into A Total Bore)

- Talk non-stop about your newborn - mostly in arguing about who it looks most like
- Brag about how quickly it learnt to walk (though everyone knows poos can't walk - unless you tie them to a string)
- Buy it designer clothes and toys though all it wants to play with is an old loo roll tube
- Boast about its first words "Splash" and "PHFLGH"- a shameless lie since all poops have only partially-developed vocal chords and cannot speak

Once The Novelty Value Of Your New Born Has Worn Off

Some new poorents never tire of their new poopie (1%). But for the rest, the drying-out factor and loss of smell leads them to ditch the dirt and poocreate yet again.

POLICE

Have a nice life, my precious.

Immediately After Delivery

Some modern women don't desire to gestate a poop for 9 hours either due to not eating enough to actually conceive a poopie, or fearing it may hamper their career (little realising that producing fine craps will raise their male boss's regard for them). For these barren bowels, there are alternatives:

- SURROGACY: paying someone else to produce a crap for you, although it's highly likely they'll selfishly want to keep the offspring.

- ADOPTION: believe it or not, there are many unwanted poopies - from mixed veg backgrounds, those that have been produced illegitimately (laxatives), or one night stands with a dodgy kebab. Most who choose adoption find it hard to bond with their adoptee.

- POO-SNATCHING: This is illoogal, but the main reason for not using this method is the chance of breaking the newborn as you snatch it from its gawping poorent.

Arsercise

IT'S TIME TO WORK THAT BUTT, BABY!

To live well into your 30s, you must look after your health, and since all doctors agree that the bottom is the most important organ, you must take extra special care of it... with a healthy diet of high fat, carbohydrates and beer and regular Arsercise – the latest fitness craze sweeping the United States of Americarse. Perform these arsercises daily and you'll see the difference in years:

THE WARM UP

WARM UP FOR 3 EARTH MINUTES WHILE YOU HYDRATE YOURSELF FULLY BEFORE WORKING OUT

GLUG GLUG GLUG

BEER

THE SQUAT

HOVER OVER TOILET SEAT AND HOLD POSITION FOR AS LONG AS IT TAKES.

THE SQUEEZE

REPEAT INDEFINITELY UNTIL YOU CAN BEAR HOLDING ON NO MORE, OR IMPLODE.

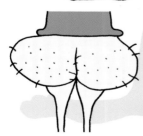

SQUEEZE!

THE PUSH OUT

FINALLY RELEASE THE BUTTOCK CHEEKS AND STRAIN. LIKE HAVING A BABY ONLY THE END RESULT IS BETTER.

PUSH!

THE GRIMACE

REMEMBER TO KEEP BREATHING REGULAR. PANTING IS FOR ADVANCED PRACTITIONERS ONLY.

THE BICEP CURL

REPEAT 1,342 TIMES UNTIL CLEANISH.

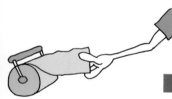
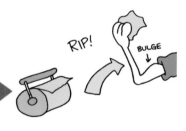

RIP!

BULGE

THE LUNGE

A GREAT UPPER BODY WORKOUT. FOR BEST RESULTS, JUST IMAGINE YOU'RE STABBING YOUR BOSS.

LOOK OUT FOR OUR VIDEO: "KYLIE DOES THE POO WORKOUT!" YES! FINALLY KYLIE REVEALS THE BUTT STRAINING SECRETS BEHIND HER PERFECT DERRIÈRE! ONLY £85.99 AT ALL BAD SHOPS.

HOW TO BAKE
THE PERFECT POO!
by Delia Jeff

Ingredients:

½ cabbage
a handful of sprouts
1 tin of baked beans
several cheap beers
salt & pepper to taste
a dash of laxatives
sweetcorn optional as it will mysteriously appear anyway

Utensils:
1 large toilet bowl (if nothing else is to hand, a urinal will suffice)
palette knife in case of sticking

Method:
Chop ingredients vaguely in mouth, mix with saliva concentrate if available, and swallow. Leave to stew in bowels for several hours at 37.4°F until aromas develop. Remove carefully from anus ring, taking care not to break it - use a palette knife if stuck and leave to cool.

Serving Suggestion:
Present as one large helping, or as individual servings.
Sprinkle with fresh quilted loo paper for a special occasion.

Seasonal Variations:
At Xmas, add turkey to the recipe for added depth and intensity.

Drinks Idea:
Wash down with half a bottle of bleach.

(serving suggestion)

Plop Psychology Quiz

What kind of shit are you? (Or save yourself the time doing this pointless quiz and ask your so-called "friends")

Question One

When you've achieved a particularly smelly poo, do you...

- a) use the air freshener before it even hits the water
- b) stay in the bog until the smell disappointingly disappears
- c) open the door, waft it, to fragrance the entire house
- d) bottle it

Question Two

If the loo roll is nearly finished, do you...

- a) waddle around the house, pants round ankles, looking for spare
- b) er, who needs loo roll?
- c) finish it, don't replace it and hide the spare...tee hee
- d) scream blue murder until emergency help arrives

AAAAAAH!

TRIP!

Question Three

You leave a skidmark in the bowl, do you...

- a) see a Rorschach ink picture
- b) clean it 2,000m times whilst gagging 3,000 times
- c) cover it with an Everest of paper, leave it and block the system
- d) "pretend" to clean it with bog brush whilst actually making it worse
  (bonus points for returning brush dirty to holder)

Question Four

You execute a turd sooo big, it won't flush, do you...

- a) perform a Bruce Lee with the bog brush
- b) call your friends, relatives and neighbours round to admire it
- c) taxidermy the beauty and mount in glass case
- d) move house

Wow! It almost looks alive.

Question Five

In public toilets, do you...

- a) let rip - making as much noise as possible
- b) pee/poo in mega slow motion to reduce noise disturbance
- c) dribble all over the seat, tee hee
- d) public toilets?!! You'd rather do it in your pants.

Question Six

A baby has done a woopsie, do you...

- a) check out the nappy contents like a scientist
- b) run round screaming like a girl when the nappy comes off
- c) what's the big deal, you crap your pants all the time
- d) congratulate the offending nipper on its wanton abandon

HISSSSS

Question Seven

If you should be so lucky to get the squits on holiday, do you...

- a) regret it, because it all happens too fast to properly enjoy it
- b) think of the money you've saved on colonic irrigation
- c) not leave your room for fear of "accidents"
- d) go on as many excursions as possible - you're an adrenalin junkie

Who needs a speed boat ?!

THPPPPPT!

Question Eight

When it comes to animal poop, do you...

- a) take a picture/home movie
- b) spend hours at the zoo just in case
- c) peek in dog litter bins for a cheap thrill
- d) pray to be reincarnated as an elephant

I'll give you a close up.

THWOP!

Scores!

4-8 points = you're so repressed, you make Queen Victoria look like a pole dancing ladyboy gimp

9-18 points = hmm, could try harder

18-25 points = full (skid)marks for effort

26-871 points = you don't honestly think we bothered to work these points out properly, do you?

POO PARTY GAMES!

BIRTHDAYS, WEDDINGS, HAMSTER FUNERALS...THROW A PARTY YOUR GUESTS WON'T BE ABLE TO FORGET - EVEN AFTER HYPNOTHERAPY!

PASS THE POO!

CEREMONIOUSLY WRAP THE SPECIAL, FRESHLY-LAID PARTY POOP IN TOILET PAPER AND VOLUNTEER TO BE THE BORE WHO DOES THE MUSIC. KEEP SCHTUM AS YOUR UNSUSPECTING GUESTS PASS ROUND THE MYSTERIOUSLY WARM PARCEL. "NO, IT ISN'T A CROISSANT" YOU TELL THEM, LAUGHING GAYLY!

Quick! Quick!

PIN THE POO ON THE I.B.S. SUFFERER

PIN THE WITHERED, FURRY TURD ON THE UPTIGHT "I'VE GOT LOTS OF FOOD ALLERGIES" IBS 'SUFFERER'. EXTRA POINTS FOR PINNING THE FOSSILISED ARTIFACT ON THE HYPOCHONDRIAC'S FACIAL ANUS.

POOSICAL STATUES!

WHEN THE TOILET WATER STOPS FLUSHING, STRIKE A GRIMACE AND FREEZE.
(MEN BE WARNED: WOMEN HAVE AN UNFAIR ADVANTAGE AS THEY ARE SKILLED
AT SQUATTING FOR HOURS IN PUBLIC INCONVENIENCES...THOUGH MEN ARE ALSO
QUITE ADEPT AT BEING IMMOBILE.)

Jeff moved!

POO DUNKING!

JOSTLE GOOD-NATUREDLY OR PUNCH YOUR WAY TO BE THE FIRST TO DUNK.
GRAB THE WHOOPSIE WITH YOUR MOUTH AND ENJOY A REFRESHING
FACIAL AT THE SAME TIME. THE WINNER GETS TB!

Got one!

BLIND MAN'S GUFF!

BE THE JILLY GOULDEN OF THE FART WORLD - SEE IF YOU CAN GUESS THE OWNER OF THE AROMA. DOUBLE POINTS IF YOU CAN GUESS WHAT THEY HAD FOR DINNER! NOTE: VICTIMS OF FOLLOW-THROUGH ARE ENTITLED TO SEEK DAMAGES. (PERSONAL INJURIES LEGISLATION CLAUSE 46, SECTION 8, PARAGRAPH 3.)

Ah yes, it's an old vintage, I'm getting cabbage notes with a soupçon of prune. It's Alf!

Yes!

 # HIDE AND REEK!

A GAME FOR ONE PLAYER ONLY. HIDE YOUR TURD IN YOUR HOST'S HOUSE AND NEVER EVER TELL THEM WHY THEIR HOUSE HAS BEEN CONDEMNED BY HEALTH AND SAFETY. WHAT A WHEEZE! (NOTE: BEST HIDING PLACE IS BEHIND A RADIATOR OR A SEXY UNDERWEAR DRAWER WHICH IS RARELY VISITED.)

Farts and Crafts projects

KILL TWO TURDS WITH ONE MOAN – RECYCLE ALL THOSE OLD LOO TUBES AND CREATE FASHIONABLE ACCESSORIES TO ENHANCE YOUR LAVATORIAL EXPERIENCE. THERE IS AN ARSETIST IN ALL OF US!

DIY GAS MASK

SLIT EMPTY LOO TUBE TO CREATE TWO FLAPS. COVER OPPOSITE END WITH CLINGFILM*. PLACE FLAP OPENING OVER NOSE AND MOUTH TO CREATE AN UN–AIRTIGHT SEAL. HOLD IN PLACE WITH HAND OR SELLOTAPE (BONUS SIDE–EFFECT: SELLOTAPE GIVES A MOUSTACHE WAXING FOR THE LADIES)

CAN'T.... .... BREATHE!

SLIT HERE   EMPTY TUBE   CLING FILM   ELASTIC BAND

*pierce to avoid suffocation. Authors accept little responsibility for maker's failure to comply with common sense.

EYE PROTECTORS

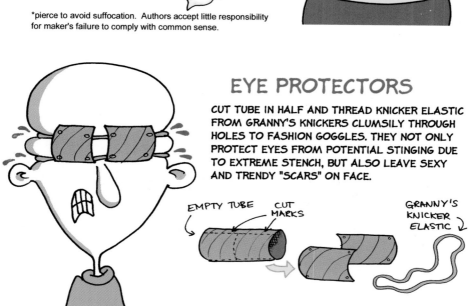

CUT TUBE IN HALF AND THREAD KNICKER ELASTIC FROM GRANNY'S KNICKERS CLUMSILY THROUGH HOLES TO FASHION GOGGLES. THEY NOT ONLY PROTECT EYES FROM POTENTIAL STINGING DUE TO EXTREME STENCH, BUT ALSO LEAVE SEXY AND TRENDY "SCARS" ON FACE.

EMPTY TUBE   CUT MARKS   GRANNY'S KNICKER ELASTIC

AROMA DISTRIBUTER

TAKE OLD MAGAZINE STUFFED BESIDE TOILET COVERED IN DUST AND GOODNESS KNOWS WHAT, AND REMOVE PAGE. FOLD INTO A FAN (HAPHAZARDLY TOWARDS THE END AS BOREDOM SETS IN) AND THEN WAFT PONG VICTORIOUSLY FOR ALL TO SAVOUR!

FOLD   FOLD   BLAH   BLAH...

THE FANFARE

EITHER COLLECT DISCARDED TUBES FOR SEVERAL WEEKS OR INSTIGATE A BOUT OF DIARRHOEA BY VISITING GRUBBY LOCAL KEBAB SHOP. FASHION TUBES INTO A TRUMPET AND HERALD THE ARRIVAL OF YOUR CHOCOLATE STAGECOACH.

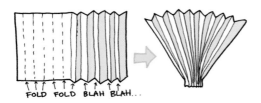

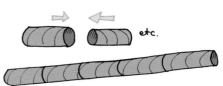

THE DUMPOLENE

WE ALL SECRETLY ENJOY THE SURPRISE OF THE SPLASHBACK – AND WHAT TURD WOULDN'T RELISH THE THRILL OF THEIR VERY OWN TRAMPOLINE. SO, YOU SCRATCH YOUR POO'S BACK AND IT CAN SCRATCH YOURS. JUST REMEMBER TO JUMP UP QUICKLY TO MARVEL AT THEIR FORWARD SOMERSAULT WITH PIKE.

POO PAL

ALL TURDS, BIG AND SMALL, ENJOY A PLAYMATE IN THE WATER. TAKE TWO SWEETCORN KERNELS, GLUE TOGETHER WITH ONE FRESHLY PICKED BOGIE AND DRAW A FACE AND WINGS TO CREATE A TINY YELLOW DUCK! AFTER ALL, SWEETCORN IS A POO'S BEST FRIEND.

CHANGING FLUMES

POOR POOS. THEY SPEND JUST SECONDS ON EARTH, PLUMMETING TO THEIR WATERY GRAVE. YOU OWE IT TO YOUR TURD TO HELP THEM MAXIMISE THEIR BRIEF EXISTENCE BY MAKING THEM THIS EXHILARATING LOG FLUME

A) CUT OLD LOO TUBES IN HALF
B) STICK TOGETHER IN SPIRAL FORMATION
C) PLACE OVER ARSE AND WEE-HEE-HEE

WEEE!

TOY-LETS

GIVE YOUR POOS A STYLISH MAKEOVER. CUT OUT THESE DECORATIVE CUTTERS AND PLACE OVER YOUR SPHINCTER TO CREATE CRAZY FUN TURD SHAPES. POOING NEED NEVER BE ANAL AGAIN!

SPOOGHETTI

THE CHOCOLATE STARFISH

THE BUTT KISSER

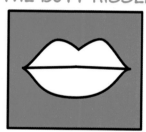

THE POOQUET

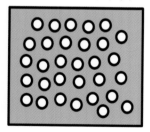

GINGERBREAD MAN

THE POODLE

LOO ROLL

Pass the minutes whilst you wait to pass the parcel with these step-by-step origami creations using simple loo paper...

ORIGAMI

"The Still Sea"

Instructions:
1. Tear off single sheet
2. Lay flat
3. Tra-la
(Difficulty rating: easy-poosy)

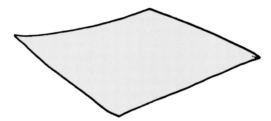

"The Yellow Squit Road"

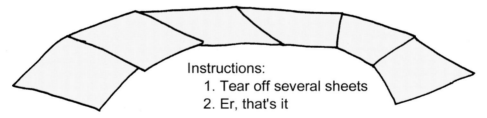

Instructions:
1. Tear off several sheets
2. Er, that's it

"The Tent"

FOLD

Instructions:
1. Tear off a sheet
2. Fold into triangle tent-shape
3. Find homeless mouse to live in it

Thankyou!

"The Carnation"

Instructions:
1. Remove several sheets from roll
2. Scrumple enthusiastically
3. Give to a loved one (or someone you've sinned against)

"The Intellectual"

Instructions:
1. Remove one sheet from roll of the poolosopher's inspiration
2. Adorn one's head with 'mortarboard'
3. Intellectualise away

"The Surgeon"

Instructions:
1. Make incision along dotted line and slit open
2. Place over mouth
3. Inhale until you turn blue

"Imaginary Popcorn Holder"

Instructions:
1. Take one sheet
2. Twist into cone shape
3. Glue in place with bogey (Can also be used to pretend to be a Womble)

"The Eiffel Tower"

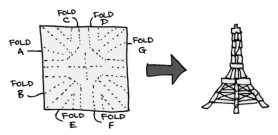

FOLD C
FOLD D
FOLD A
FOLD G
FOLD B
FOLD E
FOLD F

Instructions:
1. Fold A to B to D to C
2. Fold E to F to A to D
3. Repeat 3000 times.
4. Dur, like this is genuine.

WARNING: Thick people beware of Paper Cuts!!

The Odd Squad's
PEBBLE DASH GAME!

BUBBLE! SQUIRT!

You let out a massive fart next to someone smoking. The resulting blast sends you flying forward 4 spaces!

BOOM!!

You stop to help an old granny cross the road but the smell of poo reminds her of a story which takes her 8 hours to tell. Miss a turn.

...And my poo was eight feet long and no-one believed me and....

You pause for a second to contemplate how poo is the force which unifies us all. How, no matter what our social status or intellectual rank, we all must drop our pants and squeeze out a chocolate sausage. Miss a turn.

Last night you washed down a vindaloo with fourteen pints of lager and you have to go **NOW!** Can you run to the toilet before you ruin those new undies?!!

What you need: One dice, One marker per player (use toilet roll tubes).

How to play: First to splat their load on the loo wins!

The babe you fancy is across the street. Afraid to have her see you with squidgy pants you hide in a nearby phone box until she moves on. Miss a turn.

POO PUZZLES

Who knew poo could be this much fun?!!

D	I	A	R	R	H	O	E	A	P
S	E	U	P	M	U	B	S	E	C
T	N	F	L	O	A	T	E	R	O
I	E	A	E	B	O	A	S	T	W
N	S	E	I	C	T	P	O	L	P
K	R	C	J	I	A	L	S	I	A
D	A	E	H	E	L	T	R	U	T
U	X	S	H	I	T	E	I	G	W
M	A	N	U	R	E	A	P	O	O
P	I	L	E	S	J	R	W	W	N

Find these words in the grid:

TEAR   PLOP   TURTLEHEAD
MANURE   SHIT   POO   PILES
PEE   DUMP   DIARRHOEA
FLOATER   SHITE   FAECES
ARSE   BUM   BOAST
COWPAT   STINK

DOT TO DOT

Join the dots to discover what happens when you mix twenty beers with an extra hot vindaloo!

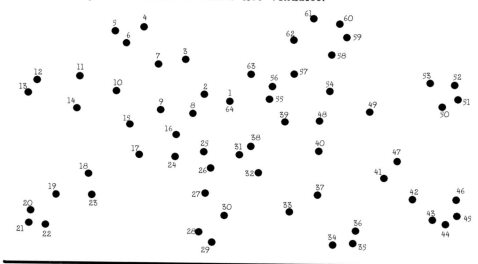

GET THE POO IN THE BOWL

Which path will take our lonely poo to his beloved home?

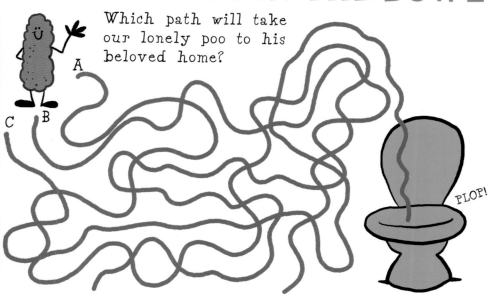

PLOP!

SPOT THE ODD ONE OUT!

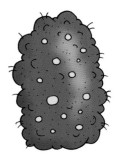 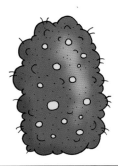 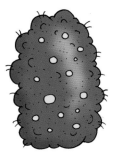 

WORD SWAP

Change the piping hot pizza into a piping hot poo in only five steps!

P	I	Z	Z	A
J	O	B	B	Y

MATCH the POO to the ANIMAL!